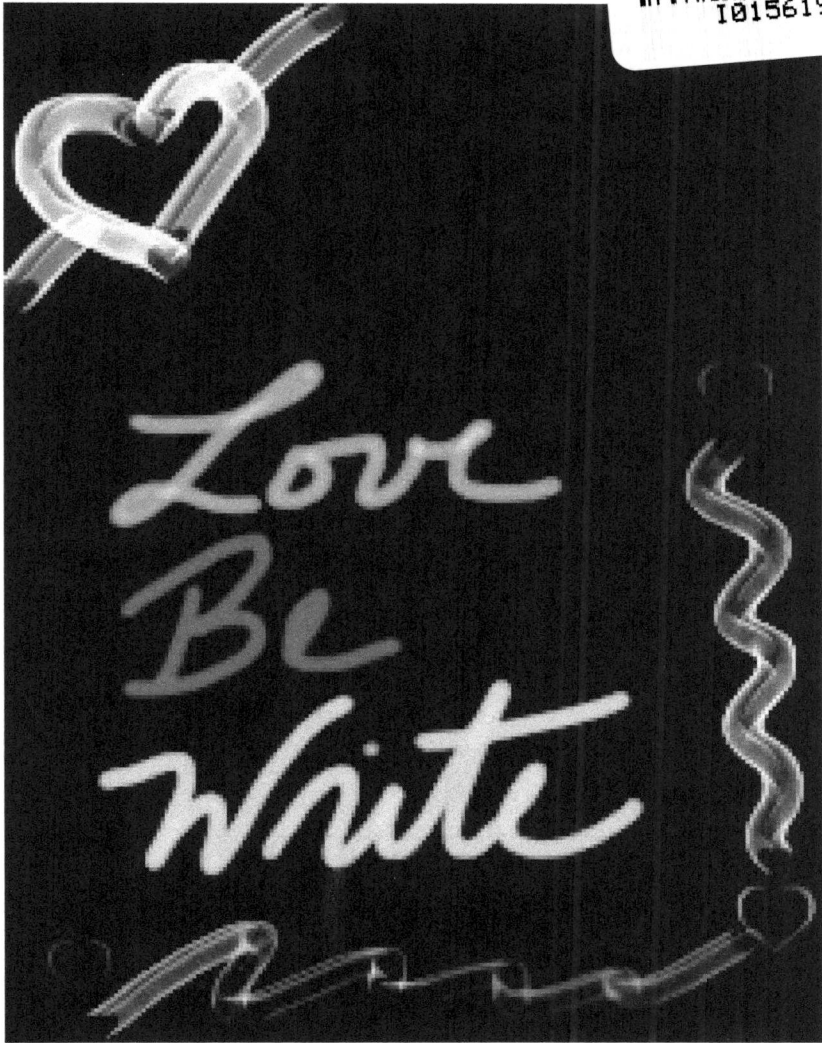

Love Be Write

vox poetica Contributor Series 2010

edited by Annmarie Lockhart

ISBN 978-1-936373-12-3

Love Be Write

vox poetica Contributor Series 2010

unbound CONTENT ✧

With much appreciation to the writers for being so generous with their gifts and the readers for being so lavish with their praise.

It began in 2009 and got even better in 2010: The Contributor Series, 4-6. The poems that appeared in the series were invited via calls for submissions sent only to writers whose work had already been published or accepted for publication at vox poetica, the idea being to create a conversation among these talented writers on a particular theme.

The fourth series was focused on love; for as many writers as signed on there were as many viewpoints. The fifth series explored identity and brought us statements of being in writers' own voices. The sixth series seemed like a trick question: write about words. What holds these themes together? The vastness of the terrain they cover. No one poem captures more than a molecule of the meaning of its big, broad, far-reaching subject.

Allow me to present these three ambitious series that know no bounds. I hope you enjoy this continuing collection of fine work by fine writers on a diverse assortment of topics.

—Annmarie Lockhart, editor

Table of Contents

Contributor Series 4: Aspects of the Elephant

Contributor Series 5: Dramatis Personae

Contributor Series 6: A Currency of Words

Contributor Series 4:
Aspects of the Elephant

To a Past Love
By Jean McLeod

I no longer measure past woes;
have stopped setting snares
to catch tiny wrongs,
flowers fill my yard.

The closer you come
the faster my heart beats,
I'll run to greet you
beneath a blue moon

arms filled with blossoms
mouth, with honey,
a hundred books
beneath our tree.

Stay 'til you're warmed
go when you're full
return if your journey allows
all is healed between us.

Failed Romance
By Stan Galloway

The little boy offers his best fire truck
and invites her to the box
where she sees the castles that he
has not built and the prince who
has not ridden to the rescue.
He says he likes the way she shows the
ribbon in her hair, meaning he likes
the way she shows the ribbon in her hair,
while she hears the one-tenth
surface to a nine-tenths depth he
won't reveal.
He reaches out to tie the shoe
string that falls loose and she
begins to list the hundred other
broken things he's failed to see, thinking
love and entropy are opposites.
He drives his cars around her,
happy that she chose to squat with him
for a time, while she wonders
why he needs her there while
he does his own thing oblivious.
Then she begins to talk and talk and he
turns his ear to her and finally says,
again, he likes the ribbon and
she turns away and leaves the box
to the shallow boy with the one-track mind.

So Who Will Teach My Sons the Dance
By Kenneth Karrer

So who will teach my
Sons
The dance?
The holding and the
Call
How to master melody at the
Heart of all
Or how it is to
Hold
But not to
Grip
To spin near fainting's
Edge
And feel that delicate, delirious
Deliquesce
But still respect the
Meter
And the time
How to rhythm subtly,
How leading is to follow.
And how it is all somewhere
Between
Demand
And
Soft suggest
And when to ask
And when
To simply allow
Her there to
Rest.

The God of Apathy
By Robert CJ Graves

I. Invocation

Tell us, Muse, of divine un-doings.
Rise from those deep wells:
those wine-dark waters,
those warm nights in the rain.

Told and retold are the old tales of castaways,
refugees drawn together on sandy shores,
and a queen who stepped self-impaled
into the pyre for love. But Muse,
we must know the truth, the ruins.

Tell of fires smothered and waste-desert shores,
and the one who really steals and steels hearts:
Love's and Rages's child who drains our souls.

II. The Forge

First, there was fire, the crippled god's brood,
a churning, jealous firestorm in his soul.
Vulcan hobbled about muttering aloud,
"My loving wife. Love!
Love? Am I a fool!"

His body flickered as he paced, hung-legged.
Visions of them boiled in his heart:
Her eyes rolled back; Mars' mouth, arrogant bloom,
curled with triumph and delight.

A Cyclops, called Altus, worked the enormous bellows,
and soon the frowning gorge glowed thousands hot.
Vulcan smashed copper into the tonguing flames
—lapping, roiling red and green, orange, blue—
until the melted metal glowed lux-purple.
Then he swirled in sun-yellow, molten tin
and alloyed the perfect bronze: tiger bright,
supple, but with tremendous tensile strength.

Altus lifted the ceramic melting-caldron
from the forge and poured the glowing bronze
into long, lost-wax casts for hair-wire,
where it cooled fast to wispy, honey rays.

Vulcan hammered and soldered the bronze strands
tightly together into a gossamer-
thin hunting net—inescapable yet invisible,
if not for its glancing dazzle-stars in the jealous firelight.

III. The Goddess' Bed

Vulcan took his airy net to the palace
where his wife kept her bed, and there they were:
Mars and Venus making love—her long, smooth legs
wrapped around him, the silk bed singing.
"Goddess of Love!" Vulcan bellowed and flung his net,
an angel's cape of motes in the dim candle flicker,
and it draped them in chains of airy, bronze gossamer.
No matter how Mars raged,
freedom would not come—the net held them tight.

Venus cooed to her husband, thinking she
knew just how to delight the old smith's ear,
but her songs only elicited a scoff.

"We'll see who's the fool now. All the gods will,"
and Vulcan called for Jove and Juno, Diana,
Apollo, Minerva, called the gods all
to witness the shame, and they gathered about
the goddess' bed, where Love and Rage lay,
chained in their fecundity.

The goddesses would not look on them
and turned their fair heads.
But the gods reveled in the chance to ogle
Venus, her naked body through the net.
Mercury, waspish messenger of Jove, said,
"I wouldn't mind being in Mars' place:
I'd feel lucky she could never escape."

The other gods agreed and laughed, but one,
Vulcan, whose face was creased with rage.
In a moment he had removed the net
and pulled Venus from the bed.
"Don't touch me!" Venus scolded
and walked out of the room.
"Make me a fool?"

Vulcan was silenced.

The gods and goddesses made their way out.
Mars was led away by disapproving Jove,
only Juno stopped to give her son a word,
but, "Oh my dear boy," was all she could say.

Vulcan picked up his net and gazed on the shape
pressed still in the bed, the disarray of sheets,
and he felt drained, no love or rage left.

IV. The Birth of Marvenus Apathius

Vulcan took the empty net back to his smithy
and dropped it in the melting-caldron,
where it collapsed shapeless as hot honey.

"Altus!" called the smith to his Cyclops servant.
"Melt this net; recast the bronze as coffin nails.
A god may not know death, but I can bury
my dead heart, for it rots now with all my love.
I'll build a coffin of ash then pull the rank organ
from my chest like a stinking, black molar.
I'll seal it in the ash box with brazen
nails of humiliated love and hate!"

Altus did as he was told. Silently,
he took the fire-bowled net to the forge
and placed it on a shelf deep in the oven
where the coals always glow hot. He brought fuel,
charcoal made of wild pistachio,
and spread it across the hungry embers.
Next he manned the bellows, forcing hot blasts.
2000 degrees and bronze melts.

Smiths of old faced agony if they slipped while casting.
But a Cyclops could drink molten bronze with little pain
or fear, and perhaps that's why Altus wasn't more careful.
The caldron slipped away from his hands,
and the hot bronze spilled, splashing in the fire.

Life is detours, collisions.

That melted dumb-bronze net, gleaming with sex,
erupted with life as it hit the hot coals.
Born was a creature of cool liquid metal,
and he rose honey-colored from the forge,
hovering above the hearth, mother-womb,
staring down at Altus, who was bowing:

"Thou art a god, obviously, honeyed one.
We Cyclopes give praise to all gods. Tell me
how I shall call you and many will be
the cattle I slaughter and smoke in your name!"

Marvenus was much like the other gods,
in body like men: two arms, two legs
two eyes, two ears, nostrils, hands, feet,
a mouth--but he was of a translucent bronze,
supple and gorgeous.

"I am Marvenus Apathius: the bronze-net
fertilized by a goddess' perfect willingness
and the raging lust of a great god,
but wombed in the burning, jealous forge.
I rise anathema to Mars and Venus,
for I've come to dull the beating of hearts.

Contributor Series 4: Aspects of the Elephant

There will be no more love and no more rage.
Worship me with rituals of apathy.
Sacrifice to me your passions, your heart."

With this, Marvenus was gone.
Altus rose and went to tell Vulcan,
who was building his heart's coffin
under the ash and pistachio trees.

His Muse Commands
By Annmarie Lockhart

"'Write more and kiss me'
are the two requests you
most often ask of me," he said.
I laughed because he was right.
So I wrote him this.

Your words are your mind,
your mouth, your body.
And I am starved
for the sound of you.

You are a force of creation,
and I am the source
of inspiration
mutual need
to speak/to hear
to write/to read.
These bodies,
yours and mine,
beautiful and alive,
lie apart and alone tonight
and for so many nights,
mute and impatient,
desert ranging between
three-day oases.

I ask my Poet,
my Servant,
my Master,
write more and kiss me
for I am starved
for the taste of you.
Desire fed page upon page,
by reading you.
Make your words
a channel of touch,
a wash cut through
uncountable miles
of parched sandy stretches.
Keep kisses skimming
our spaces intimate,
spilling from your lips
and pouring love like rain
down these bodies
on these pages
through these
storm-built
gullies.

For I am starved sick
with need to read
the poetry
of you.

Ladies Get New Names When They Marry
By Frank Cavano

Ladies get new names when they marry.
Sighs and smoking thighs bring forth one
then another. But one dies in the war over
there and another in the wars over here.

Oh, my love, let us wipe away these tears,
        lock our loins and love away
        the Night 'til someone comes
        to give you back your name.

Excerpt From the Diary of a Man Growing Old (December 20, 2009)
By Neil Ellman

Cleaning out my closet
I came upon an old sports coat
Harris Tweed
The color of Coney Island sand in the rain
That I had purchased more than forty years before
Collars like stretching wings
On the 1960 Chevrolet on which I learned to drive.

How I love that coat
(and the car as well)
Its shoulders made me seem more athletic
Than I ever was
More stylish than I could ever be.

You can't discard the one you love
Or give it to Good Will
Where buyers paying pennies
Could never understand the majesty
of woven wool
its history, my own —
And now a bit too large
And slightly frayed,
But so am I.

Said my wife, "It's me or that old coat!"
And I stood silently
Wondering what to choose.

Love Continues
By James G Piatt

Boyish blond hair
Graying and thin
Once strong fingers
Now bony and frail
A heart crying out
To the child within
A soul trying to recall
A vanishing tale
A mind seeking
For answers to love
An old man searching
For reasons to be
Weary hands reaching
For his loving wife
Lean arms encircling
Her thin body
Sitting together
Her head on his chest
The best of life
Still in their grasp
His wife gives him
A loving embrace
Their aged love still an
Unbreakable clasp

Now that I know
By Karen Schindler

it's hard to get what you want
til you know what it is
now that I know
what I have always desired
I can see myself shifting toward getting it
funny how that happens

Anemones
By Lisa Marie Basile

You must mulch your people like roses.

The flower, in pieces.
Its petals next to the curled foot
        of the table.

I pick them up, I hang
them so the blood runs
        to their heads.
Keep them in the dark,
I plant more.

You will remember this years from now.
It is the same with people:
        bright, dark.
When they fall,
you will collect them
you will remember
        their colour.

Jenna
By John Sherer

Her face is gone

She is pulchritude
Short, slender, light
Short hair, wide eyes

Her face is gone

I once knew it
I once did not know her

Here I sit
As I try to recall
And all that comes
Is who she is

Who she is
Is not a face
She is inside
The gone, embraced

A Cactus Grows in the Desert
By BR Belletryst

Weather, and a bird,
how dependent, cactus.

Lifecycles of the strange;
the simple desert between them.

Twenty years in the making, a bloom,
the chance, one chance, one life.

Grown steadily from roots clinging
for water, for nourishment, for affection.

Growing prickles and spines and thicker
each year, wasting efforts to fight the air.

That same energy could propagate,
could bloom many flowers, but won't.

"I was given a promise. I was given a feather."
And the hummingbird's tale unknown.

How well adjusted must one and one be
to make it through this desert, together?

This species relies on one bird, in one instant,
to change its life, forever.

What tale is it, if the avian rejects?
What of the bird and the plotline, then?

Did it fly to Vegas to gamble away fortunes?
Did it have children and "settle down"?

Did it tell those baby birdies of the time
when it knew commitment, and didn't show?

The cactus, with forty years left,
no longer worried about propagation, thinks.

Did he, like all birds, seek to fly away?
Or simply, did he oversleep?

Last petal fell, last tear was shed,
the desert, thoughts, surround.

Sentiment's Chowder
By KJ Hannah Greenberg

Long distance lovers, all
Doilies and belvederes,
Like sweet, European fish
Served with ketchup.

Local friends, in contrast,
Accept stewed heads,
Braised flanks,
Sometimes even sentiment's chowder.

Asexual BFF
By Gianluca D'Elia

Looks like we just broke up
We fought about a lot of stuff
But I still remember you
It's pretty difficult not to
And I just realized
I don't need a woman or a man
By my side

But I'd like to be your
Asexual best friend
I will text you all night
But I can't give fashion advice
Like a gay best friend would

And I'm not straight either
And I'm certainly not bi
And never again will I be your guy
However I don't want this
To be the end
I want to be your asexual best friend
Forever ...

Our Volition Was in Not Turning
By Ray Sharp

Scraps of paper
lifted on a careless wind,
these are my verses tonight.
You came to me so—

the familiar face on the
peeling wheatpaste poster
blown across the square,
come alive at my feet,

deft motion of fate's blind impulse.
This wind was not of our doing.
Our volition was in not turning,
in being that shape in the flow.

Take my hand, you said,
step with me into this landscape,
let us tumble like leaves, let us curl
like tendriled smoke.

It is the same with this poem—
it found me on a windy night,
and when I did not turn away,
that was the beginning of love.

My Companion Piece
By Bryan Borland

At the funeral they called him my companion,
which made him sound less
like my husband than my pet,
my friend with the furry belly
I instinctively rub. These two weeks
he's been the guide dog
to my blindness. I'd have run
off bridges too
if not for his steady hands
as buffers, his muscular arms
when I wake up too early,
and we cry,
but together.

Remnants
By Kim Klugh

Shadows gather on a January afternoon;
I give in to hazy memories of
a cheap guitar,
a torn bus ticket
and clinging regrets
of a song, unsung.

Virtual Love
By Joan McNerney

A
long
slim
poem
full of hyperbole
and alliteration drifted
into the wrong e-mail box.
There she met an erudite
rich text format manual.
They became attached.
Her fleeting metaphors
lifting his technical jargon.
They were a word couple
spinning through cyberspace
giddy with inappropriate syllables.

Hunger Strike
By Ivan Jenson

I am going
on a hungry
for love strike
where I will
refuse all
nourishment
until something
is finally done
about the rampant
loneliness that
plagues the earth
I want to
raise awareness
for the millions
who pang
needlessly
against the walls
of isolation
and bang
endlessly
on the shut
doors of intimacy
who hunt
fruitlessly
through want ads
only wanting
to be wanted

this silent
but deadly
scourge is
infiltrating
the cities
and yet the only
cure is for
others to come
into contact
with the infected
loners with
the only known
vaccine
the anti
body
is a
warm body
to hold onto
all through the night

For Valentine's Day
By Jeanette Cheezum

For Valentine's Day he made me his wife
the next year we gave new life.
He gave me jewelry for each of his little
girls. Little did he know he was my
pearl.

Sun up, sun down, I always knew where
he could be found. Together we made
it through the years, more laughter than
tears.

Our girls enjoyed life until someone
made them their wife. Those men
couldn't compare to their Daddy.

I saved all my valentines, one by one.
Now that he's in heaven I cherish them
all. Take out the box and clean the cover
remembering him and no other.

I Have No Memory of Love
By R Martin Basden

I have no memory of love
but the harbor of your arms
and the shelter given daily
in your smile

Time does not exist
without you by my side
even time before the vows
that marked us one
before the world
isn't measured in its nakedness

For I am clothed in you
even named as you
as a couplet in a poem
cannot stand on just one line
there is no me
without you
to make the whole.

For My Growing Twin Sons
By John Lee Clark

What surprised me the most
when I first touched
my premature twin sons
was how close my palms
could get to their hearts
thrumming against tender cages.

Their skin too sensitive to stroke,
I just held them close,
chest against heaving chest,
almost heart to heart,
and I breathed close to tears,
hoping they would not die.

I hoped not against hope,
knowing that if they lived
their bodies would grow
more secretive of their hearts,
followed by other secrets
making them only themselves.

No, I hoped for hope,
that they may live and grow,
even if it is a growing distance
from me, but so they know
and hold close other hearts
hoping they would not die.

Hearts
By Mariah Boone

The heart-shaped leaves are from no tree I can see
Dark and dry
They come on some wet wind to crumble in our yard
No colors on South Texas leaves
They have no flaming hospice, only
Green, brown, dust

My stepfather, when he was the doctor that dated my mother
Brought me bags of color
from New England
Red, yellow, orange leaves
He brought me a snowball in an ice chest
Courting me with things I'd never seen

The Silence of You
By Bobbie Troy

sometimes i wish
i could suck the silence
from the air
then wrap it around you
and hope that you
invite me in

Dreams of Ramona
By Larry Blazek

You met at the old
House on the highway
Made love in your old room
Explained that the house
Was sold years ago
Was demolished and made
Into a parking lot
But you return now and then

Match
By Sarah Endo

In the blue corner we have
the welter of countless regulations:
Younger daughter gets brown hairbrush
with the lighter writing on it
Older daughter gets brown hairbrush
with the darker writing on it
Hair shall only be cut in the bathroom
And then only over a towel

But in the red corner, the weight
of countless steps, around and round
dancing, covering up, tying and untying gloves
I could weigh 500 pounds on the moon
and be beautiful to you
gentle cutman, splinter man
Ding, ding
It's a knockout

Contributor Series 5: Dramatis Personae

Man Made
By Ivan Jenson

I am always on exhibit
you can walk around me
you can touch me
you can read up about me
you can take note of the year
I was created
clearly I am an
artifact
of my time
and I have my place
and the fact
is I just stand here
standing for something
while
you are the critic
and the connoisseur
you either admire
the craftsmanship
that went into
making me who I am
or maybe you
prefer
that Greek adonis
over there
but let me warn you
that one
has a chip on his shoulder
and is as cold
as stone

A Hungry Wife
By Cassie Premo Steele

1.

The joy I feel
when I touch
your hip
in the dark
is the knowledge
that my body
is bread
and you can eat
this simple meal
and be satisfied.

2.

Taste the time
we have together.
It is not long.
Nothing is.

3.

I want more
I want to fill
to be full
to be filled
to be.

4.

In my dream
I saw people starving.
They wanted bread
every day—
only bread.

5.

I want bread
and basil,
bread and chocolate,
bread and butter,
bread and wine.
Am I selfish?

6.

This hunger
of knowing
there must be more
keeps me moving
toward the unseen
source.

7.

Sometimes I feel
I've had enough
and we sleep
soundly.

8.
Faith is knowing
I will want more
in the morning.

9.
I am
your joy
and this is
my livelihood.
We need
to invent
words
for this.

10.
I am
a hungry
wife.

Wonder
By Karen Schindler

I am a spring green shoot
pushing through the soil
warmed by the sun
nourished by the earth
entranced by the moon
seduced by bees and butterflies
I am kitten noses, puppy toes,
baby's first steps
I am joy personified
and each passing moment
renews my breathlessness

First Impressions
By Grace Burns

They met at a party
at the start of their senior year in college.
He thought she was a geek.
She, in turn, labeled him a snob.
They kept their distance from each other,
as their invisible shields.
He secretly snickered at her black outfits and
neon yellow Converse high top sneakers.
She secretly snickered at his apparent bad taste
in clothing and women.

They stumbled into each other
at a dance at the start of second semester.
Their inhibitions had been washed away
by a steady stream of beer and cocktails.
They danced and talked, joked and belly laughed,
allowing the rising tide of this new attraction
to swirl around them and
carry them off to God-knows-where.
He drove her home and
squeezed her arm good night.
I want you to be part of my life.
She felt the gentle pressure of his warm hand.
I want you to be part of mine.

Fast forward twenty years—
They have built a busy life together
since the day they looked
beyond their first impressions.
Drinking and dancing have been replaced
with career-building and bill-paying.
They are lovers who have matured
into heads of a bustling household.
The attention they had generously given
to each other is now diverted
to their children, interests and obligations.
And still, sitting together in their minivan,
he'll squeeze her arm
as their kids chirp like busy chickens,
en route to God-knows-where.
I want you to be part of my life.
She'll feel the gentle pressure of his warm hand.
I want you to be part of mine.

One Man I Stand
By Nate Spears

A tear falls from my eye
I drop to my knees and
Bow my head
I pray to the Lord.
So much chaos
In the world I live in.
Sometimes I feel it's just me.

One man
I stand
Alone.

Ode to Everyday Heroes
By Mark Gooch

Snow falling fast, the wind starts to howl,
Driveway is full, cars are snowed in.
What is that sound?
After the task, the driveway is clear.

Flames eat the wood, billows of smoke reach the sky,
A swish! And then the flames just go out.
The guy in pajamas goes back in his house.

The phone starts to ring, Central Dispatch Request:
A car has flipped over, prepare for the worst.
He arrives on the scene; she's a bit dazed,
He picks up her stuff, arranges a tow.

Leak in the roof, repairs are needed,
Furnace is broken, the pump has no prime.
There's a knock on the door, someone appears
Armed with tools and willing to share.
Soon everything is fixed, he smiles and disappears.

When the time comes to pass
And the end has drawn near,
Then and only then
My true identity will be clear.
Written on the headstone, for everyone to read:
Here lies a friend, neighbor, and Good Samaritan
Who dedicated his life for the sake of his peers.

vox poetica

Inner Lives
By Bob Christin

That scruffy bearded homeless
man pushing a cart of broken
dreams stares out at the world
in a trance, eyes unseeing,
pointed straight ahead to
protect himself from scorn,
side glances of discomfort.
His feelings locked or missing.
He is independent, a person
fully human in God's image.

When I look at his eyes closed
to my peering in, I see myself,
my scruffy, bearded spiritual
life accepting arrogantly my
cart of fulfilled dreams, my
comforts of every day without
even a nod to my benefactors
who pushed and shoved me
from nothing to the riches
I have enjoyed. My side glances
are rarely focused on the angels
who carried me on their wings
to safe living rooms and libraries
and love. Looking at this man
I scorn not him but my neglect,
my indifference, my aversion
to discomfort. I say not the
arrogant *There but for the
grace of God*, but more
humbly, *Is it I, Lord?*

56

Contributor Series 5: Dramatis Personae

untitled
By Manny Beltran

A flash of light stole the street
A swift blow mumbled the night
Spit found its new home ...
on my cheek
on my nose
on my lips

The sirens sang a repetitive song
Deep within my unconscious ocean ...
"Faggot!"
"Faggot!"
"Faggot!"

A calculated kick took my breath
And left me unable to react as a man
The patrons of life continued on ...
Unconcerned about my state
Unconcerned about my life
Unconcerned about my truth

There was no Jesus to save me
In a moment of solitude I was broken ...
Scarred and broken
Scared and ashamed
Scared and dead

Trinity
By Veronica Dangerfield

The scream was silent at first.
Wife and Mother turned in alarm
at the loud tremor: Woman escaped.
Wife screamed, a door slammed shut.
"Mother, run! Get the kids! Their lives are at stake!"
Mother ran praying "Lord! Help me Jesus!"

They screamed in sync as Woman
possessed entered in absolute rage,
violence and destruction bent.
"You two are despicable," she spit.
"Wife, your supplicant desire to please,
waiting on the likes of a man—A MAN!
YOU MAKE ME SICK."

"Mother, Mother," she mocked,
"Nasty little homeless people, YOUR children? Your children?
You must be insane!
Do you really love those beastly kids?
You give and they suck more and more.
How can you LIVE like that, you sacrificial whore?"

"Lost, alone, sick and tired
I die not once but twice a day.
My heart, my soul, our body abandoned
for a square meal and 401K?
Caring, sharing, for what I might ask?
For Life, Career, and Love of a Man?
You can all kiss my ass!

I trusted you Mother and Wife,
but you bitches were weak.
You live here like you got it good.
Vacate this place!
You locked me in this jail cell
and sucked my life blood dry.
Out of my sight!
You're both gonna die."

"Die? Die?" asked the indignant Wife.
"You should be appreciative.
Sheltered, clothed, and fed,
what is your problem, yet again?
I have sacrificed in your stead.
Self-preservation is the first law of man.
Don't you remember what Darwin said?
Without me to provide for your selfish ass,
you're the one who would be dead!"

"I am already dead, been dead for years,
trying to resurrect, I'm ready to feel
all the spirit in the laws of love.
My heart is bruised, my soul is shrunk,
time is traveling in light years.
My youth, my body, my spirit shriveled
for family and a life miserable in my hand
to add to the value and length of the days
of all the treasured people I love
but mostly cannot stand."

No Contest
By Frank Cavano

The thing I am battles
      with the thing I know
        I am
which, in turn, does nothing
      and happily for Me
        loves
today the thinking thing I'm
      not.

I Am
By Ailill

I am
a dream dreaming up a new song
in the stillness before the dawn
to celebrate the beginning of day,
awakening to my place as a rising flame.

I become
a reflection inspired
by the light of another fire,
sustained by earth's leaves, air's breath,
the poetry of this life moving ahead
to keep up with the tic toc of the clock
beating to the rhythms of noon day sun,
and the heat of the hectic city streets.

A cool wind that blows in the afternoon thunder
and drums up early evening showers,
weeping rain drops from the sky into these eyes.
The dusk that unfolds windows into the soul.

Evening's contemplation
seeking wisdom
from ancient runes by the light of the moon,
feeling as if life has just arrived.

Weariness, tucking this body into bed at night,
losing sense of space and time,
drifting off into another beginning,
coming around again as
I am.

The Operator
By Joan McNerney

With such a pleasant voice so sincere
and trusting (a female of course).
She was automated and kept on kept on kept on
apologizing how she did not get it right.

Mangling my unfortunate last name
'til finally it became mammary. I am
not an udder breast person. It's bad enough
being Irish! Was she hinting I was mammal
as in whale? She sounded so thin.

Her call back was also unreasonable.
What was wrong with my Yes?
After four times, I considered disconnecting
my phone. Finally I pressed the right button
and our conversation abruptly ended.

The DeSoto
By Joseph Murphy

The 10-year-old sat up to see over the dash,
Imagining the engine's sound.

September 1959: summer kids gone;
Gift and soda shops closed; the island's beaches
Reclaimed by gulls.

The car had been sold; time to move.

This would be his final chance
To marvel at its dials.

Death had come quickly. Grandmother
Walked in, said: "He's gone."

The boy had come to see himself
As a figurine.

Glued to a bottled ship's deck.

But sitting in the driver's seat
He seemed life size:
Holding the wheel's worn grooves,
Just as another had.

Identity
By Chris G Vaillancourt

I have been
my father's son;
my mother's son;
my grandparents' grandson;
my sister's brother;
my wife's husband;
my children's father.

I have been a child;
a student;
a poet;
an artist;
a teacher;
a parent;
a labourer;
an employee;
a social insurance number.

Now I am wondering where I am?
What is "me"?

I seem awash in
various labels,
a variety of tags
that have been
attached to me.
Each is a role to play
that supposedly defines
what I am.

Sometimes I want to disrupt
every
identity I am
compelled to play.

Upset the apple cart.

Open my wallet
and
spill out every
piece of paper that
identifies me.

If I throw away my
birth certificate,
does it mean
I have never been born?

If I burn my Social Insurance Card,
does it mean
I have ceased to exist?

Who am I?
How do I belong in this
mist of roles and perceptions?

I'm not sure anymore
I really know
who I am supposed to be.
Does this mean that I
am nothing?
Nothing, without a
label to purify me?

My Identity
By James G Piatt

Who are you
The beautiful poetess asked
Seeking to peek inside my soul
I am that which is unknown even
To myself I tell her
I am yesterday and tomorrow
I am happiness and sorrow
I am the son of my father
And the father of my son
I am learned yet I am uninformed
I experience heart aches and sadness
And darkness in my mind
When I witness injustice
My anger flares at man's malevolence
And his haughty and cold arrogance
My feelings are worn on my sleeve
Yet I am as hard as nails
I am soft and have a loving heart
Yet I am strong and tenacious
I desire to be great and yet
Spurn greatly the spotlight
I am a multifaceted dichotomy
I am good and I am evil
I am a clear window to truth
And an open door to ennui
I am that which is in my ancient genes
And I am that which is inside my mind
I am at times an opaque prism
Reflecting only darkness

Refracting back peace and light
At times I am a kind and gentle soul
At other times I have a ruthless tongue
I am sure of myself in all things
Yet I am also insecure
I shed salty tears when I rage
And smile warmly in my serenity
I am warm hearted toward humanity
Yet I can be calloused toward individuals
I love animals birds flowers and bees
I love little children and caring people
I abhor bigotry condescension and ignorance
I cannot tolerate meanness or spite
I fight mightily for the underdog
And for truth to prevail
Once with power and status
And now just with my pen
Dear poetess I guess in all honesty
I am actually just a simple man
Who accidentally became a poet

How Do Rivers Hide Their Tears
By Bobbie Troy

when night turns the corner
and becomes morning
the back of my mind inevitably stirs

with musings on the day
the complexities and the mysteries of life
trying to find the simplicity within

i wish i never cease
to think and dream

but most of all i wish
i never cease to wonder

how do rivers hide their tears?
how do children hide their fears?
how does old age hide its years?
how do rivers hide their tears?

Sisterhood of the Butterfly
By Jeanette Cheezum

I release a balloon and a butterfly
to find my sisters wherever they are.
To bring them strength, love, and
maturity in times of happiness
and sorrow. I cherish you sisters
go fly and be free.

A-head
By Alice Shapiro

Beating footprints over concrete
leave marks and shadows
if we turn to look.
The neck, curious as Lot's wife
commands reversal
and possible blockage to a pleasant walk.
The head, that fragile instrument of peace
or evil
guides and reasons,
soothes, abuses
invests, invites, deletes.
Mine in particular is king
or queen subordinating limbs
and organs, feet
to do its bidding.

I am my head.
It is sometimes red and wrathful
green and cool
it takes me where it wants to
an everlasting tool
like driver's education school.
I cannot turn it off
even if it acts the Fool.
I plan to take it with me
in its spirit body
when a head no longer rules
this solitary earthly journey.

Especially Borges
By Ray Sharp

I woke last night on the living room floor
confused about the moon and the orientation of windows

uncertain even of my right hand and left
and if my dog were a god.

Would Borges have known
if he were the same man from day to day?

Betsy the Barn Cow: A Suffragette's Lament
By KJ Hannah Greenberg

Here I quieten sad and blue,
I, a cow, who just can't moo.
Cud I form. Tail I shake,
But bovine noise, I barely make.

My milk's supreme; the cream's rich, yellow.
I'd swap that stuff for one full bellow,
Solely one note, simply one sound,
Only one teensy, ear-shattering round.

I'm tired of tether, I abhor cold machines,
It's time to earn rights by some other means.
My children are hungry, plus I've no ungulate fun.
Stupid bulls claim the pastures, the pear tree, the sun.

Maybe a stampede, perhaps a long strike,
Better yet, I could low far into the night.
If only my voice would boom this one time
I'd reclaim the farmyard, restore all that's mine.

Phantom Limbs of Family Trees
By Bryan Borland

I am history's orphaned
sibling, the retold story
of the men in my family
and our phantom brothers.
Granddaddy named my mother
after Sergeant Morley Joe Colvin,
323rd Bomber Squadron,
91st Bomber Group,
a nosedive casualty, he
holds our place
in the Eastern hemisphere.
Marshall Borland also
went down in flames, my paternal
grandfather's brother whose
house and bones melted
and merged with the delta soil.
I was myself a younger brother
for thirteen years, before
lungs met clot and Glenn Colvin Borland
evaporated. Now my uncle
knows the emptiness,
a severed limb, my father gone,
the arm you lose, the missing half
that sways in the wind.

Sojourn
By Gianluca D'Elia

I am sojourn
In this society
This world is not
Where I was meant to be
This 6-foot-tall body
Is just temporary

I am free spirited
And I'm just tired of narrow
minded people
I like to do stupid things sometimes
Because I can INSPIRE
by making someone laugh today
In this depressed world

And today is a perfect day to
Fly away
The sun and the sky
Are my brother and sister
And tonight is the night
That I'll leave this place behind
My wings aren't strong yet
But I can fly

All I feel is strange
In a perfect world,
I am a nightingale
In a golden cage
Who longs to be set FREE

I'm SOJOURN in this society
I know nothing lasts forever
So I'll leave this world eventually
I'm tired of them labeling me
And telling me who I am
Just let me be myself

Average
By John Sherer

I am rich
Easily amused
Far from needy
Lonely, but not alone
I can smile
And, often, can agree
A little bit of money
And comfort bought cheaply
Not much to content
Or making excitement
Acting out of place
Thrills both me and them
Thread is curious
And drawing language
What seems to be abundant
Is more than enough
Life must be my choice
Else it would not make sense
I choose to obey
My master is my slave
Pays little
But has so much
Serving, saving, securing himself
I save and secure and serve myself
But stress, not I, this thing called wealth
Because I can have some too
With more time to spend with you
With less to spend on you

Long Division
By Rae Spencer

Long have humans sought conflict
Rejected each other
With words that maim community
Barriers buried in pronouns

Enmeshed in massive groups of they
He and she live apart from you and I

He follows a spiritual path
Into places you cannot understand
And she lives in a neighborhood
Many miles away from me

They earn more or less than you
And disagree with my politics

A different gender
A different race
Or named by the million descriptors
That bind and blind

Mostly they are outside our experience
An entire section of humanity lost

In some other frame of reference
You are they and I am them
And everyone is separated
By pronouns that exclude

Miracles come in smaller words
That include we and us

The Voice of God
By Sandra Forte-Nickenig

When God speaks I hear
Miriam and her timbrels
and the roar of bearded patriarchs
waiting for Moses to descend Mt. Sinai.

When Jesus speaks I hear
a chorus of disciples
praising his name while
Jezebel pursues forgiveness.

When Allah speaks I hear
sheepherders praying in the desert
through the shaft of blinding light
seeking water for a parched soul.

When Buddha speaks I hear
the murmur of a hymn
and the faint plashing in the pool
where lotus blossoms promise peace.

When the Great Spirit speaks I hear
the bones of my ancestors
beating a tom-tom as their faces
flash in a star-filled sky.

When Mother Earth speaks I hear
a cascading waterfall and
I dance through whispering meadows
in search of a lover.

When my Higher Power speaks I hear
the voices of friends
who sit in a circle and laugh
at the ironies of reality.

Yet if truth be told,
all gods sound remarkably like
the voice of a Jewish woman searching
to discover the mystery of the universe.

A Sestina for Little Picasso
By Brad Nelson

My son's favorite color—red,
but he also likes orange,
prefers colored pencils yellow,
wants his crayons green,
likes to watercolor with blue,
and loves to finger paint in purple.

Giraffes should be purple
spotted in red
with five legs of blue—
or is it six? Orange
eyes crossed, staring at a green
tongue drooping to grass grown yellow.

Yes, son, grass can be yellow,
and I'm sure some trees are purple.
I have seen a house that is green
all around with roof red,
matching doors of orange,
but who is this monster painted blue?

Yes, your mother is sometimes blue.
Yes, she does have beautiful yellow
hair—mixed with orange
mixed with purple
mixed with ... What is this red
thing? Is this the dog in green?

Well I hope the new baby is not green,
for your mother's sake. Blue
would not be much better. Red?
There may be some. Yellow
hair like yours? Purple
beard? I know this man in orange.

Though a slightly darker orange,
maybe, and eyes of green,
holding hands with a little purple
boy with big blue
eyes and yellow
hair, cheeks flushed red.

Shirt smeared red and face spattered orange,
A little boy, yellow brush clenched in green-
smeared fingers painting a blue paradise purple.

I am
By Jimmi Ware-Phillips

I am "that" poet
She who preaches peace
Praying for innocents to be released
I am but a leaf on the tree of history
With strong roots, tall boots and ephemeral youth
Let me share some truth
I am a black redhead with brown eyes
I hate racism and lies
I love family and global ties
I weep for those in pain
I twice gave back their name
I know from whence I came
I adore Dr. Seuss and summer rain
I was touched by an angel
I'm not the same
I knew heartache, heartbreak
Stood at the Arctic Ocean and a great lake
I was hugged by Nikki Giovanni,
Danny Glover, not too often by my mother
I once wanted to be a dancer
Long before my father had cancer
The hardest word I've ever heard was
Good bye
I prefer to shed tears of joy
When I cry

Love is as amazing as the freckles on my face
He is leather and I am lace
We appreciate this Blessing
Humbled by grace
I am beginning to see my mother in the mirror
Wisdom has a way of making life clearer
I still hold my dreams near
Luckily
I know why I am here
Warrior Princess, Nubian queen
Never the imagine in your magazine
Friend, sister, mother, daughter
When they thirst I am water
No matter where you come from
Show me a smile
It all works out
After a while
Never doubt
Whether I read
Green Eggs and Ham
It inspired the Poet I am.

Untitled
By BR Belletryst

I.
Bottle fed from Mother Goose's pinion;
I romped in Dahl's and Seuss' playground.

Frequent trips to libraries for paper
hugs from literary friends

Matilda, Stargirl,
Julie and her wolves,

I grew up with Brian Robeson,
and shrunk again with Alice's potion.

II.
Then fed with fire from Bradbury, Poe,
Dickinson, and Frost,

I broke down with Plath, cried
for Algernon, and grew jaded with Orwell.

In midst of depression with Zooey and Frannie,
Cisneros whispered to me:

"You must always keep writing,
it will keep you free."

And just like Esperanza,
I didn't understand.

III.
I fed on voices
Shelley, Wilde, Byron, etc.

Until one day, with pen and paper,
All I could think were echoes.

IV.
Whispers once soothing seemed
claustrophobic.

I felt their inky arms in my chest,
grasping along my spine, entombing me.

My paper family, so close,
I became origami.

V.
Their dry rustlings, their musings
and fussings.

Mashing fingers on keys,
scratching pen on paper, marker on arm.

Impassioned scribbling, maddened
and unhearing, I stormed.

I wrote, and understood.
In writing, all other voices were silenced.

VI.
Their page-built arms rocketed me forward,
tossed me into the air just as

the first scream, the first echo
of a newborn in the world,

passed from my body to the page,
and melded with their clouds of breathy echoes.

Circling Creativity
By Jeanette Gallagher

I am the I am waiting to be born
Still connected to my mother's womb
Attempting to leave the breast
That holds no milk for me

Waiting for contractions to force me
From constrictions of a crowded belly
Circling within spirals of creativity
Afraid to enter the chaos of being

Scared of being swallowed by a vast void
Of stillness so sacred filled with such joy
Where soul whispers let go just be
Know the I am, the I am of me

Fearing in the universe within
I will find all I have to offer
Are empty circles posing as words
That expose the impostor in me

Narrator
By Annmarie Lockhart

You know
that I was never meant for mute.
My voice was meant to fly,
my words were meant to sing,
and I was meant to be
the stream of consciousness
that moves the story
from beginning to end
and bends the babble
through all the twists and turns
along the way.

Contributor Series 6:
A Currency of Words

Words of Delirium
By Clarissa McFairy

my life is an overloaded handbag
at the moment
with several pantomimes going on

in different compartments
and some emotional stuff
that has been zipped up too long

starting to seep out
like words from the mouth
of a delirious patient

Blue
By Nicole Yurcaba

yellow swirling green combining perfectly
indigo peacock's feathers
crisp wide-open Wyoming skies
Hank Williams' "Long Gone Lonesome Blues"
Pacific, Atlantic oceans
Denim—light and dark
Teal, cerulean, various shades
Union Blue versus Confederate Gray

blue-ticked coonhound howling at October's moon
wheat Blue Moon beer, honey-spiked
Turquoise—
rings, earrings, bracelets, studs, belts, Native American
Aquamarine—
March birthstone, a gem.

Blue—
cool, sophisticated wrinkled tarp covering split firewood—
must be the color of the blues

Blue—
Planter's peanut can, gold lettering, dancing Mr. Peanut
Blue-ice, Busch Light can ... I feel—
blue—
three days and not one single message.

Blue—
Oyster Cult playing in a blue '96 Dodge Dakota SLT pick-up
that he traded for an '02 Silver Dodge Dakota—the worst
mistake ever.

Turning blue—
holding breath, puffing cheeks—"I FUCKING SCREAMED
UNTIL I WAS BLUE IN THE FACE!" What a perfect color for
you ...

Blue must be the color of—
        tears, cold, fleece, suffocation, bruises, frozen, freezing,
gel pens, water, sky, ink, panties, jeans, eyes, pens, polka dots,
running streaks, Febreze spray bottles, lampshades, curtains,
dyes, nail polish, Bug Juice, pick-ups, wagons, light specials,
cooling flames, dying ...
        —the Union but we wore Confederate Gray ...

Forbidden
By Gianluca D'Elia

I feel so compelled to write
It's been so many days
Or has it been months, years?
Everything was destroyed
In the fire and the explosions
Guns and bombs and helicopters
Their sound everlasting
Left us with nothing but ashes

I cannot find a pen nor paper
Amidst the destruction
Not even a splinter

I take a rock
And etch my words into the dirt
Making an imprint on the soil
For all the feet that may walk it.

Words of Life
By Bobbie Troy

in the furious tide of thoughts
words are born
erupting like a child
from the womb
never to be yours again
but still having a semblance of you

you grow the words
and guide them
from infancy to maturity
then leave them for posterity

Ode to Nice
By Christine Tapson

I'm proud of you.

Charged, sentenced, executed
Only you.

Every breath you take is bound to be sweet
Crisp, clean, and happy.
Pretty.

We can move away from pain and fear
Towards pleasure and love.
The destination might seem the same.

Underrated, discriminated against, banned.
Exiled from our vocabularies and our prose
While encompassing such vast potential.

Fat, self-important words like *pintadera* and *petasus*
Samskara and *thrombolysis*
Hog the stage.

I like you. You're fine. I'll embrace you.

In the Name of All That's Holy
By Jeanette Gallagher

In a quaint, quiescent
Countryside called Montvale
The villagers thrive

As one in a state of grace
Deserving as God's chosen
Countrymen where righteous

Souls abide and love endures
Exemplar ethics in all that's holy
Virtue paragons: alabaster white.

Scandal rocks sacred ground
When life's flow shames
One's family name

While daughter delivers
Female child good townsmen
Christen bastard

Decide what else will do
But seal her fate and
Desecrate certificate of birth
By stamp, Illegitimate.

The A-Word
By Grace Burns

anger
absolute
acrimony
acknowledge
attack
advance
Autism

Words
By Mildred Speidel

She said yes
He said no
Then a maybe
would soon
echo

I love you so
Well I love you
Then what's
the problem
with "I do"

I'm not sure
Well neither
am I
So that ended
it all
She did not reply

Silence is a word
that everyone can
hear

It never finds a voice
but its message is so
clear

Word for Word
By Ivan Jenson

Earth
means the
world to me
and I love
love
and hate
hate
but
could
care less
for carelessness
and negativity
has a negative
effect on me
I don't
want to
want
and it
hurts
to hurt

so I
walk
the walk
and talk
the talk
take
each
day
a day
at a time
and
it ain't
over
til it's
over
and the plus-sized
lady sings

Gifts Not Errors
(for Sophie)
By Louis Gallo

You will not remember when
you saw *leddo*, never yellow,
and the integers refused to toll
in rigid gongs, eternally fixed,
but danced ... one, two, five,
three, ten, eight, and on toward
intinity, the secret number
no one knew about but you.
You will not remember my stories
but you may *nemember* every word.
You warned me once
as I pruned ivy from our porch
that I might catch a radish.
                    "No way, Jose,"
I said, which caught you off guard.
Brooding in envy, you waited your chance,
and when it came, stomped into the room
and cried *Not for good nothing, Jose*,
finger wagging, as mine wags.
You ate *hamuka-ka-kas* and held
not your horses but your hearts
while the horses made their *manora*.
If I compiled your perfect mistakes
into a shabby notebook, forgive me.
They were gifts, not errors.

I lost the notebook, I confess,
the way we always lose things
we need or love. Still,
I'd like to weave your magic words
into a necklace you could wear
once you've finally eased into
the cold equations of our tongue —
to remind you always of that first
limitless, lovely world.
I will, for now, *nemember* for you.
I'll hold my hearts, braid your *leddo* hair
and fry a juicy *hamuka-ka-ka*.
Together may we choke
the fatal radish
until it sings.

Fission
By Ray Sharp

Written words are stable atoms, elemental units
of meaning that bond in thought molecules,
but when we talk we emit radioactive isotopes
prone to degradation, hot charges that burn
under the skin. How long is the half-life
of a lie? How strong is a lethal dose of insult?
Could you stand to wear the weight of lead
or would you sooner brave the fallout, naked
to the chain reaction of a critical mass of words?

You Call Me Caro Mio
By Salvatore Buttaci

Under the sheets of passion you call me caro mio,
But once love melts into final throbs and last breaths,
Your eyes glazed like impromptu tabloid snapshots,
You turn your naked back to me, say how the night
Is finally here after a hectic day of scheduled madness.
I hear from my side of this nocturnal territory, your voice
Fuzzy as wool in dreamscapes, words in a tunnel,
Something uttered just before the runner leaps into dream.
Too soon your gentle snoring playfully pokes the walls
And I lie here, arms behind my head, staring upward
At heaven from where we have just returned, and think
To myself those charged words you called me:
I run them through my mind like a prayer: *caro mio*,
Dear one, dear one. And then your hand touches my face,
I feel alive again. Connected this way, I surrender
To the tug of sleep's hands; your words, sleep's voice.

Sin of Omission
By Kim Klugh

What needs to be said
is that I regret
my silence
that I did not speak up
that I did not say *stop*

breathe

take a step back

that my courage froze full in my throat
so in the end I was just like the rest
waiting for someone else to make a move
to make it cease
to halt the crossfire
to utter, *enough*

what needs to be said
in the aftermath
is that I am sorry
you ended up a casualty
but for one word
I could have voiced

Apology
By Stan Galloway

Give me back the words I spoke
that stung you like a hailstone
in the rain. I don't know
where they came from,
what imp urged
the battle in my tongue,
some malevolent,
invisible,
unwanted spirit.

Give them back so I can grind them
into powder and dispose of them
in one grand flush
or mad triumphant flash of fireworks,
this time for good.

Give them back
because they did not
represent my heart—
a heated tongue
extended from a neutral brain,
a moaning of insensible wind
in a Rocky Mountain storm,
destructive,
meaning nothing.

Give me back the words—
oh—if you could only
give me back the words.

Verbal Destruction and Restoration
By Ryan Haack

With my words, I destroy you.

Little slices at first, like cardstock papercuts to the skin
between your fingers, for which there is no special term.

An insult and you feel like an ant, crushed underneath
a giant foot; even worse when you don't see it coming.

Then I yell and call you a name, maybe spit out a curse
and you're like a pea crushed between my finger and thumb.

On and on, verbal punches to the gut, striking your soul
with relentless precision, singularly focused on the win.

I laugh and you're gone.

I make you feel like you're nothing.

But, you are something.

You are everything.

In the mirror I see the lumberjack who has chopped you down;
the bruiser, the beast, the brute, the bastard; the darkness.

My hope is to restore that which I have destroyed, to heal that
which I have hurt, to spark the fire I have extinguished.

To somehow raise back to life that which I have killed.

With my words, I'll lay a foundation of trust, solid and
unshakable;
erect walls that are sturdy, with windows to see into your soul.

I'll encourage and delight you, supply you with all you need
to decorate your home how you would like: pink, of course.

I'll secure the roof, your protection complete. Your house, your
home, your place of refuge. And I will come back, meekly,
knocking.

Asking softly if I may enter. Will you have me back? Will
you invite me in? Will you laugh with me again?

Will you smile authentically, crinkling your nose? Will you
let me hold you? Will you forgive me and allow me to stay?

Will you?

I let my words purr like a cat
By Laura Zucca-Scott

I let my words purr like a cat
Rolling in comfort and unspoken love
Hoping understanding would break the night

Hope is never easy to come by
Sought after, corruptible and pure,
A child jumping in his father's arms

Words are overrated
Chimeras of sophisticated times
Dangerous and simple

If only one word could be spoken
I hope it would speak of love
Slow and caring, and new

Like a cat purring in my arms

Aloha
By Jessie Carty

Insert Key. Turn. Pull. Push. Locked. The ritual of safety. Drop keys on table. Open and close the refrigerator door, thinking 1—this time I'll see the light go off 2—this time there will be something new inside. Sesame Street logic. Abierto. Cerrado. Sounds close to Alberto and Grenada. A person. A country. A man. A plan. A canal. Panama. In the morning reverse it all. Closed as a starting point. A palindrome of consistency. Goodbye and Hello. Aloha.

What Remains
By Rae Spencer

Bone, of course
Or the stone echoes of bone
And children
Always there are children
To symbolize our guilt
For the things we couldn't change
And hope
Wrung from what we did

Empty spider husks
Wafted into corners
With a clot of hair
And a few crumbs
That might have been food
Or not

And windows
Mostly broken
But some not
With just enough dust
To obscure the details
Of what else might remain
On the other side

An unknown balance of cats
Abandoned
Or maybe never loved at all
Furtive, feral shadows
Fleet with the urge to survive

And everywhere there are words
Scribbled and scrawled in diaries
Painted on underpasses
Stamped into books
Shouted once and left to echo forever
On the wind

Enough words to hold all of us
And still describe what remains

Handle
By Paul Hostovsky

Because I don't have anything to hold onto,
because I don't have a Bible
or a family ancestor or two
the way others seem to
when the going gets
a little bumpy
as they say in airplanes
flying around
up in the firmament,
a word that's probably
in the Bible—not bumpy—
bumpy isn't in the Bible,
though it probably should be—
but firmament, a word that
sounds like what it isn't,
almost certainly
is in the Bible somewhere.
Therefore I hold onto
the words. You might even say
I harp on them
because of the musical
connotation which I love,
harp being the biggest
instrument in the whole ensemble,
a piece of furniture practically—
you might even stay afloat on a harp
if the ensemble ever went down,
if it ever went under. I know
the words can't save me.

But aren't they the most interesting things
in the Universe, which is the one
Verse, the one great Poem?
I would rather say spelunking
than go spelunking any day.
In the beginning was the word, they say.
But I think they got it backwards. The word
came after the thing. The thing came first.
And then somebody, Adam probably,
gave it a name, gave it a handle.
But in the end, you have to let go
of everything. Even the words, even your own
name — lay it down like a broken
thing laid down beside the broken thing itself.

lights like fencers heads
By Mark William Jackson

outside a train station fixed to a wall
there are lights like heads of fencers,
masked and slightly bowed.

I saw this as an interesting observation,
but you really have to see them
for yourself.

as I looked at them
I struggled to describe
them in mental construction.

then thought of the pleasure
and relief when you hit
the right word and
like silver halide salts exposed
the image is captured.

this is not a poem about
lights like fencers heads

this is the Love.
this is the Sanity.
this is the Healing.

Wordsilk
By PD Lyons

reminding me of words like
border line
crescent coyote
ancient timbers
polished smooth as kisses
paradise
abandoned eyes of shipwrecked sailors
myriad pin prick suns
flightless birds
something Spanish that you said along a twilight turquoise
Ishmael to Ishmael
all the nights we've ever known
not bothering the quiet.

Words Upon a Plaque
By James G Piatt

Words upon a plaque

Silent memos
Of our lives consisting
Of countless
Inward and outward
Battles lost and won

Lives etched
On slabs of wood
With unmemorable
Words engraved
On thin yellow
Metal foil

A once existence
That can never be
Erased or rewritten
Ghastly words
Outlining forever
Our subsistence

Bland sentences
Haunting the present
Cold metal epitaphs
Constant reminders
What someone thought
Was important in our lives

Sharp barbs pricked
With silent laughter
The telltale remains
Of an invented life
Insincere words
Now forever cast

How one detests
All of those whereases
On a wooden tablet
Hanging silently
In some second hand store's
Dusty back room

Fame
By Ian Gammie

There was silver in my jar
that I pocketed for a paper.
No one reads them these days,
but I saw your piece, it said
looking for fame.
Now I'm swiping plastic cards,
stacking up hours to buy broken
adventures on turbo engine planes.
Then I'll get a parallel plot,
Hello, I'm _____, I'll say,
and I think we'd get on ok.
I followed the paper trail to find
your name: It's pretty wrapped in ink.
And I think that was bold,
it's tough never to be heard.
I'm sure you've ran your ad before,
hoping someone would pick it up
and put silver in your pocket.
Promise me, when you've made it,
you'll let it all burn away,
until you find what you're looking for;
then say that was never the goal,
you always wanted something more.

Phases
By Guy Traiber

I searched for G-D
in the synagogue; parchments and swaying men.

I searched for G-D
by the riverbank; naked
men dipping and spraying.

On the high mountains I
found one fat man
and a guru with an airplane.

I searched for G-D
in the lowest place on earth;
Stain of light between tired coals.

I searched for G-D
on the bookshelves, upper row;
Buddha, Descartes, and the Book of Nothing
the Bible, the Qur'an, the Bible Two.

I moved them all one shelf down
and placed instead books of literature:
Alterman, Cohen, Borland
and an anthology of red poetry.

I open a new notebook
first line
I am searching for god in the words.

Licorice Cement: Revisited
By Alice Shapiro

Once I wrote nonsense
jabberwocky, jargon, words
juxtaposed to make a poem.

When they awarded me
thirty pieces of silver
I tried to fake it again.

Failing
I now offer up that anomaly
one rare stab at
language, rhythm
an awkward push
to make words say
what they do not mean
an infant plan to have the world
conform to chaos.

Licorice cement
is hanging past daffodil
stovepipes.

On rice-cracker books
are bands rugging shoes,
and postcard perfumes
leafing glasses.

I stamp window bricks
in snowcones.

Air comes beyond
Eucalyptus coffins,
and brushes
broom on.*

Always somewhat odd
I reminisce on the power of the tongue
and look to a future
when an equally odd youth will pen
a sequel verse I could not birth.

*from *Poetry Connoisseur* ©1985, Alice Shapiro

A Harmonic Gallop
By Julie Ellinger Hunt

a waterfall of selective adjectives
ignites and unfolds
precludes to another world at another time
like a harmonic gallop.

The story ignites a dust storm
picking up pronouns and pretense, then
freefalls into a tidal
pool.
Floating with fragmented sentences
and title phrases.

a poetic chaos.

Lip-reading while listening
like a lexis harbor.
(Expressionism
is everywhere)
the marina lulls the buoyant boats,
as the terminology gets caught up
in the seaweed.

Terms sink fast unlike
the syllable sea horses
the next word can ride upon.

Words
By Hugh Fox

Remembering back to obsessive Fox back
when I was in high school, everyone else
out base- and footballing it, me at home
in my cubbyhole bedroom in our apartment
on the far South Side (Chatham) in Chicago,
reading all of Aldous Huxley's and James Joyce's
fiction, St. Augustine's Confessions, Jorge Luis
Borges (in Spanish) ... when I'd find a word I didn't
know, keeping notebooks, writing them down, then
dictionarying them, let's try Hemingway and T.S.
Eliot, Ezra Pound ... brain-notebook ... writing sixty
years later, going into my usual word-trances and
here they come again ... where did THAT come from,
or, or, or ... memory gone for everything else, but
the word garden somehow still in bloom.

Poison Pen
By Jean McLeod

Words lie on my paper
like dead fish:
blackened bones
meaningless motes.
Smelling of iodine
and rot,
they straggle, strive
ring with slander
slither
through my fingers
onto a sullied page
roiling like
seas before a slattern
storm.

Unruly heathens,
they slash
and leave me bleeding.

Women cover their ears,
press tight
against buildings.

Men shutter
their eyes,
cover their genitals,
cross the street
so my words
will not splash
them.

The Descent
By Joseph Murphy

As evening drew up I lingered outside,
Waiting for what might jump
From mind to page.

I must wake the slumbering body of these words.

A stirring has begun!

At my feet, a willful phase
Reshapes a patch of light:
In a thought or two, it's become a door
I swing open.

Down I go.

I enter a grand chamber:
Clouds protrude from roots; flesh and leaf
Reflect identical images.

Shaping my language into a ladder, I descend further.

It's quiet this far down. Still. Lovely.
I just breathe. Perfect.

But I must return.
I'm not yet ready for such peace. I can't stop
Pestering my words: tapping them
On the shoulder; sorting
Through their memories; unfolding
Their maps.

Poet and Lyricist: A Love Poem
By BR Belletryst

1.
You caught my ear, the first time you spoke
a stressed consonant here and there.

You used words I rarely hear,
and I was unaware.

You gave me your name, your heart and
your tongue.

I gave you my story,
a song unsung.

2.
You helped me, lover, to find my throat,
many a night and morning.

You bit into it, and drew my doubt,
and swallowed all my warnings.

A two-year program, a two-year affair,
was all I needed to poetically swear

that tangled words, that clips and phrases
have given me grace that
flows and amazes.

That, in two years, our love has lingered,
and in two years, I have fingered

at the edges of confidence and art
while you steadily helped

pump my heart.

Lightning Poetry
By Maxwell Baumbach

in my dream
lightning struck
outside the mouths
of ordinary beings
turning the words they spoke
into poetry

it would be
beautiful
if
we could do that
in reality
on our own

Is It a Poem?

By Frank Cavano

Is it a poem or a prose poem?
If a prose poem, is it prose or
poetry? Is the verse free or too
expensive to be published? Do
you like poetry to rhyme? And
what do you call it if it doesn't?
Oh, that's right, free verse! But
are there enough metaphors and
do you comprehend all of them?
You do! And is that good or does
it bespeak a lack of cleverness on
the part of the poet? Not so much
alliteration now! Is it a real poem?

Does it qualify as a sonnet? Strict
criteria or loose? Always iambs or
just sometimes? The last two lines
indented, right? Hell, maybe I will
try to write a villanelle and end up
completely confused. Haiku! Did
someone sneeze? Well, God bless!

Is it a poem, a real poem? Let the
literati decide. I merely ask that it
be written by a Heart. For can the
rose be a rose absent all its thorns?

Poetic Insomnia
By Kenneth Karrer

They come to me in
p-i-e-c-e-s

They sit beside my ear
and nip
and gnaw
and chew
Symbolisms onomatopoeic
(hidden meanings to eschew)
wasted on a pillowed
Head.

Lightly, slightly, they
alliterate
and often rhyme and
come
(again quite late)
and claim their time.

Soon if well behaved
They form in
l
i
n
e
s

and stanzas
and march to proper
meter
(yes, iambs if they're noble)
Still others serve
to
only clutter and produce
sonombulatory mutter
(move, damned Spot, this is my "best bed")

And as this bard begins
to snore
some wise trochee
SHOUTS
"what's all this meta for?!"

Word's Worth
By William C Ross

Scriptures on cathedral walls.
Graffiti scrawls on restroom stalls.
A word's true worth is the thought behind it,
And poetry is where you find it.

Tasting Words
By Neil Ellman

Say a word
Listen to its bouquet
Swirl it in a glass
And sip it slow
Let it linger on the tongue.

Repeat the sound
And savor it
As if it were a wine
Full and round
With hints of spice
Plums and bramble fruit.

Drink the word
A letter at a time
And know the taste
Of poetry.

The Contributors

Ailill is a teacher and a traveler.

R Martin Basden, a retired engineer, lives in Norfolk VA with his wife Kay. He enjoys singing for his friends, digging in the dirt, and writing poems, short stories, memoirs, and critiques. Prodded to submit by fellow writers, he has been published repeatedly in church and local anthologies. Thanks to *vox poetica*, he scattered a handful of poems into cyberspace in 2009 and 2010.

Lisa Marie Basile has been published in several literary journals including *Word Riot*, *elimae*, *Moon Milk Review*, *Willows Wept Review*, *The Foundling Review*, and others. She is the founding editor of *Caper Literary Journal* and the author of a full-length collection and an e-chapbook: *A Decent Voodoo* (Cervena Barva Press, 2012) and *White Spiders* (Gold Wake Press, 2010). She works for PEN American Center's Prison Writing Program and is a member of The Poetry Brothel, an arts organization. She is an MFA candidate at The New School.

Maxwell Baumbach makes a mean bowl of ramen. He also edits the *Heavy Hands Ink* publication and watches unhealthy amounts of Sports Center. His first chapbook, *Suburban Rhythm*, was published by cc&d through Scars Publications in September 2010 and his second, *You're Welcome*, is forthcoming from Alternating Current Press. His work has appeared at a bunch of places so google it.

BR Belletryst is a gay writer and poet based in central Ohio. He has been writing professionally for several years and his work has been published in several online literary journals. Visit his blog at brbelletryst.wordpress.com.

Manny Beltran is a visual artist and writer who lives in New Jersey. His art and poetry has appeared at various places. Manny is currently working on a revised edition of his first book and a second book as well.

Larry Blazek was born in northern Indiana but moved to the southern part because the climate is better suited to cycling and land is cheap. He has published *Opossom Holler Tarot* since 1983 and is always looking for submissions. His work has been published in journals such as *Five Fishes*, *Front*, *Mountain Focus Art*, and *vox poetica*.

Mariah Boone is a mother, teacher, social worker, and writer living in Corpus Christi TX with her husband and 2 daughters. To read more from Mariah visit her blog: www.lonestarmablog.blogspot.com.

Bryan Borland is a multi-time Pushcart-nominated poet from Little Rock AR. His first book, *My Life as Adam*, was published by his own Sibling Rivalry Press and a second book, *The Hanky Code* (cowritten with Stephen Mills) is forthcoming from Lethe Press. He is the editor of *Assaracus*, the only print journal in the world dedicated exclusively to gay men's poetry. The poems appearing in this anthology are from his project *Less Fortunate Pirates: Poems from the First Year Without My Father*.

Grace Burns lives in New Jersey and is the mother of 2 children. She is an automation and validation engineer, technical writer, mobile DJ, and creative writer. She is also very tired.

Salvatore Buttaci retired from teaching in 2007 and now spends every day writing poems, articles, letters, stories, and blog postings. His work has appeared in publications such as *The New York Times*, *USA Today*, *Christian Science Monitor*, *Cats Magazine*, and others. He has conducted writing workshops and been featured at various poetry readings. His next book, *200 Flashing Shorts*, is forthcoming in 2011. Visit his blog: salvatorebuttaci.spruz.com.

Jessie Carty is the author of 3 poetry collections but she also chisels away at prose in between teaching at RCCC in Concord NC. You can find her taking photos and editing Referential Magazine or blogging at www.jessiecarty.com, when her 4 rescued cats get off the keyboard.

Frank Cavano is a retired physician who writes poetry inspired by powerful feelings, thoughts, or images. His work touches on being human, healing, and spirituality. His words have been published in both literary and medical contexts. His poetry has appeared in journals such as *Blood and Thunder*, *The Penwood Review*, and *Indigo Rising*.

Jeanette Cheezum has been published in 3 *vox poetica* anthologies to date and is a devoted reader of vox. Her work has been published on numerous online sites and she has completed 3 novels. You can see a list of her publications at www.hamptonroads.org.

Bob Christin is a retired English professor (Ohio State University, Pace University, New York University Notre Dame). He has taught creative writing at the Adult Learning Center in Virginia Beach for 10+ years. He is the founder and lead mentor of The Albright Poets. His work has been widely published and he is writing a book-length literary memoir.

John Lee Clark was born deaf and became blind in adolescence. His work has appeared in many publications including *The Chronicle of Higher Education*, *The Hollins Critic*, *McSweeneys*, *Poetry*, and *The Seneca Review*. His chapbook of poems is *Suddenly Slow* (Handtype Press, 2008) and he edited the anthology *Deaf American Poetry* (Gallaudet University Press, 2009). He lives in Minnesota with his wife, the deaf cartoonist Adrean Clark and their 3 sons.

Veronica Dangerfield is a comedian, teacher, poet, traveler, and self-proclaimed salsa queen. Her creativity and quirkiness barely keep her viably employed. She is the mother of 3 but mothers all children. She was not born but dropped off in the US and raised in Japan, the basis for her one-woman play Unidentified. Born to teach, preach, and make people laugh, Veronica does all that in Oakland CA.

Gianluca D'Elia is a teenage writer and actor on a quest for world domination (more like outreach of love). He has been writing since he was 9. He is the 3rd youngest contributor to *vox poetica* to date and has made his name known at *Caper Journal*. Gianluca also writes songs and he is currently working on a novel called Heal. He is a devoted Kerli fan, a hippie, a singer, and a closeted chocolate addict.

Neil Ellman is a retired educator living and writing in New Jersey. He is widely published with 5 chapbooks to his credit; the latest is *Mirrors of Miró: Ekphrastic Reflections of the Art of Joan Miró* (Flutter Press, 2011).

Sarah Endo lives in Massachusetts with her family. She sometimes finds herself wordless with wonder at life and love, yet tries to find words anyway.

Sandra Forte-Nickenig is the 1st-generation American child of Russian immigrants. Born in Brooklyn, she graduated from Brooklyn College as an English major specializing in critical analysis of poetry. Before retiring she was as an executive for an international self-help group. She published articles, reports, and poetry. Her writing explores the immigrant experience, love and loss, and the interconnectedness of man, woman, and nature. She lives in Virginia Beach with her husband and is a member of The Albright Poets.

Hugh Fox is dying of prostate cancer which is spreading all over his body. His books *Depths and Dragons* and *Immortal Jaguar* will be published by SkyLight in early 2011 and his poetry book *Approaching* was released by Grey Sparrow Press. Hugh has been nominated for a Pulitzer Prize.

Jeanette Gallagher moved to Virginia Beach at age 10 and grew up in an ocean-front family-operated hotel. She is a retired therapist who worked at Tidewater Psychiatric Institution and Center for Behavioral Medicine. She belongs to The Albright Poets and Hampton Roads Writers.

Louis Gallo's 7th poetry volume, *All in a Night's Work* is soon to release. His publication credits include *Glimmer Train, Missouri Review, New Orleans Review*, *Bartleby-Snopes*, *Raving Dove*, and others. He teaches writing and literature at Radford University in Virginia.

Stan Galloway teaches English at Bridgewater College in Virginia. His book *The Teenage Tarzan* was released by McFarland & Co in January 2010. His poetry has appeared in *vox poetica*, *Caper Literary Journal*, *Loch Raven Review*, *The Atrium*, and *WestWard Quarterly*.

Ian Gammie is studying creative writing at UEA. His work has appeared in several publications including *Neon* and *Poetry Quarterly*.

Mark Gooch is the business manager of a mid-sized corporation in Lansing MI. A graduate of Bentley School Systems in Burton, he lives in Clio with his wife Pam. His poetry began with the suggestion of friends.

Robert CJ Graves's work can be seen in literary journals including *Leaf Garden*, *Anastomoo*, *Chiron Review*, *Eclectic Flash*, *Eleutheria*, *WestWard Quarterly*, *Danse Macabre*, and *vox poetica*. A former bartender and sports writer, he holds a PhD in English (rhetoric and writing) from Bowling Green and an MFA in creative writing (poetry) from Wichita State.

KJ Hannah Greenberg and her hibernaculum of imaginary hedgehogs roam the verbal hinterlands. Sylvan creatures to a one, they fashion verse from leaves, shiny bugs, and marshmallow fluff. Their poetry can be found at *Cantaraville*, *Language and Culture Magazine*, *The New Vilna Review*, and *Poetry Superhighway*. Hannah has read submissions for *Sotto Voce* and was nominated for a Pushcart Prize by *The Shine Journal*.

Ryan Haack is a husband, father, pastor, and writer in Verona WI.

Paul Hostovsky has been featured at *Poetry Daily*, *Verse Daily*, *Best of the Net* (2008, 2009), *The Writer's Almanac*, and *The Pushcart Prize XXXIII*. His new book of poems, *Mostly*, is forthcoming from Main Street Rag.

Julie Ellinger Hunt lives in northern New Jersey with her 2 crazy sons and even crazier husband. She swears they are part alien (wink). After completing a writing program at University of Delaware, she published 30+ poems. Her work has been featured in *New York Quarterly*, *Ascent*

Aspirations, *Poetry Speaks*, *Poetry Repairs*, *The Momo Reader*, *Carcinogenic Poetry*, *Wired Ruby*, and *Caper Journal*. Her 2nd poetry book, *In New Jersey*, is due in early 2011 from unbound CONTENT.

Mark William Jackson is a Sydney-based writer who has appeared in various print and online journals including *Popshot*, *Miscellaneous Voices*, *Blue Crow*, *The Diamond & the Thief*, and *Going Down Swinging*. Visit his blog: markwmjackson.wordpress.com.

Ivan Jenson's work has been widely published in the US and UK and he has been recognized for his Pop Art. His Absolut Jenson painting was featured in *Art News*, and *Art in America*. His poems have appeared in *Word Riot*, *Zygote in My Coffee*, *Camroc Press Review*, *Alternative Reel Poets Corner*, *Poetry Super Highway*, *Word Catalyst*, *Hidden City Quarterly*, and others. He writes novels and poetry in Grand Rapids MI. Visit his website: www.ivanjenson.com.

Kenneth Karrer is a retired public school teacher currently working for the Texas Education Agency. He is a member of Austin Poets at Large and his work has appeared in numerous journals.

Kim Klugh writes from Lancaster PA. She is a part-time freelancer with articles in publications including *BusinessWoman*, *"b" magazine*, *Central PA Magazine*, *Susquehanna Life*, and *Lancaster City Living*. Her work was included in the anthology *My Dad Is My Hero* (Adams Media). Her poems have appeared at *vox poetica* and *Eclectic Flash*.

Annmarie Lockhart is the founding editor of *vox poetica*, an online literary salon dedicated to bringing poetry into the everyday. She has been reading and writing since she could read and write.

PD Lyons recently returned to the US after living abroad for 12 years. Adjusting well enough. His newest book is *Caribu & Sister Stones* (Lapwing Press Belfast). Visit his blog: pdlyons.wordpress.com.

Clarissa McFairy, aka Clare van der Gaast, is a South African journalist living in Cape Town. Her hobbies are painting, writing short stories and French poetry. Clarissa's work has appeared in South African anthologies, *vox poetica*, and in 2 *vox poetica* anthologies.

Jean McLeod's work has appeared in journals such as *Reader's Digest*, *Family Circle*, *Roux Journal*, *Concise Delights*, *Spinetinglers*, *Leaf Garden*, and others. She is a Pushcart Prize nominee, 2nd-prize winner of the Christine Sparks Award for Poetry, and winner of the Agnes L Braganza Award for Prose. Her short story *Flowers for Charlie* was made into a grand-prize winning movie (Hiroshima Film Festival, 1997).

Joan McNerney's poetry has been published in *Seven Circle Press*, *Dinner with the Muse*, *Blueline*, *63 channels*, *Spectrum*, and Bright Spring Press anthologies. She has had 4 books published by fine literary presses; her newest is *Having Lunch with the Sky* (APD, Albany). She has read at National Arts Club, McNay Art Institute, and other venues.

Joseph Murphy is a professional editor and writer in Michigan. His work has been published by journals such as *Poetry Quarterly*, *The Tower Journal*, and *The Broad River Review*. Joseph is the poetry editor for *Halfway Down the Stairs*.

Brad Nelson is a former US Army interrogator and backyard samurai. He earned an MFA in Creative Writing from National University and serves as publisher and chief editor at Eclectic Flash. Brad lives and writes in Arizona, though he sorely misses Tennessee.

James G Piatt earned his BS and MA from California State Polytechnic University and a PhD from Brigham Young University. He is a retired college professor. His work can be found at *Contemporary American Voices*, *Word Catalyst Magazine*, *Apollo's Lyre*, *Caper Journal*, *vox poetica*, *Front Porch Review*, *A Handful of Stones*, *Autumn Leaves,* and others.

William C Ross feels that his different jobs in the industries of broadcasting, advertising, public relations, and government administration reveal how strongly he values the written and spoken word. Poetry is an abiding passion of his and his hobby in retirement; his specialty is "versifying" the dictionary.com Word of the Day.

Karen Schindler writes even when she's not writing. A passionate lover of life, she lives with gleeful abandon and pulls others into her wake. Karen has been published at *Eclectic Flash*, *vox poetica*, *WeirdYear*, *52 Stitches*, *Ink Node*, *Negative Suck*, and other ezines and anthologies. Visit her blog: miscellaneousyammering.blogspot.com/.

Alice Shapiro is a Pushcart Prize and Georgia Author of the Year nominee and the author of 3 poetry books. Her verse tragedy will be produced at the Douglasville Literary Festival in July 2011. She is executive producer of American Poet–GA Sports, a TV series in which poets compete for a book contract. www.poetrytv.org.

Ray Sharp composes poems while running, biking, skiing, and race-walking the forested hills of Michigan's Upper Peninsula, writes them in composition books, and types them with his 2 index fingers. His work can be seen at *Astropoetica*, *Caper Journal*, *Eclectic Flash*, *Ink Node*, *qarrtsiluni*, Spark, *Referential Magazine*, and *vox poetica*. Visit his blog: raysharp.wordpress.com.

John Sherer is a recent graduate of Trinity College in Hartford CT. Since graduating he has worked in litigation support, lived in NYC, moved back to Connecticut, begun to interview to be a paralegal in NYC, and is generally trying to figure out what to do with the rest of his life wading through all that nonfiction.

Nate Spears was born in Jacksonville FL, where he still lives. He is a young inspirational poet and writer with the vision to change the world via his writing. Nate began writing short stories that amazed his teachers when he was 7. Now Nate is spreading some inspiration to smile with his debut book of poetry, *Inspiration 2 Smile*. Nate is a proud author with unbound CONTENT and he is working on his 2nd book.

Rae Spencer is a writer and veterinarian living in Virginia. Her poems have been published in *Wild Goose Poetry Review*, *Raven Images*, *Grey Sparrow Journal*, *vox poetica*, *Bolts of Silk*, *The Glass Coin*, and elsewhere. Her work was nominated for a Pushcart Prize in 2009 and 2010. She can be found online at www.raespencer.com.

Mildred Speidel is retired and lives in Chesapeake VA. She loves poetry and has enjoyed meeting new friends via the internet. She is a mother, grandmother, and great-grandmother: proud and busy.

Cassie Premo Steele is a Pushcart Prize nominated poet, writer, and creativity coach who lives along a beautiful creek in South Carolina. She is the author of 6 books, including the recent novel *Shamrock & Lotus* (All Things That Matter Press, 2010) and *This is how honey runs* (unbound CONTENT, 2010). She is an inspiring guide during the creative process and works with clients in person and long distance. Visit her web site: www.cassiepremosteele.com.

Christine Tapson is an educational psychologist/remedial therapist who has turned to farming indigenous African cattle for stud in her retirement. She lives in a remote rural area of the Eastern Cape in South Africa where she indulges her dream of living in and being surrounded by nature.

Guy Traiber was born in Israel. He has spent the last decade traveling extensively throughout India, Southeast Asia, and Europe. For the past 2 years he has lived in South Germany studying sociology and political science and trying to put into words what his heart has seen.

Bobbie Troy is a freelance technical editor/writer by day; by night she writes flash fiction, poetry, and original fairy tales with a 21st century twist. Her poetry and fairy tales appear online and in print in journals such as *Concise Delights*, *Caper Literary Journal*, *Haiku Ramblings*, *Leaf Garden*, *vox poetica*, *Journal of Liberal Arts and Education*, SPARK, and others. Her work was nominated for a Pushcart Prize in 2009 and her fairy tale play *Sasha and the Tree of Sorrows* will be produced in 2011.

Chris G Vaillancourt has had 200+ poems published in journals internationally. A series of his chapbooks was published by Four Winds Press and his 5th collection of poetry *Sky Stained With Tones of Red* is forthcoming from unbound CONTENT. He is the founder and editor of the ezine *P&W* (triangularduck.bravehost.com).

Jimmi Ware-Phillips is a poet with a purpose. She uses her gifts to uplift the hopes of young people in Alaska. She is a Covenant House volunteer for homeless teens. Her organization, Black Feather P.O.E.T.S., works to prevent suicide by producing public service announcements as part of the Reasons to Live campaign. Jimmi loves the beautiful tranquility of living in Alaska and believes in giving back.

Nicole Yurcaba is a 2009 graduate of Bridgewater College in Virginia, where she majored in her one true love — English. Her work can be seen at *vox poetica*, Bridgewater College's *Philomathean*, Mary Baldwin College's *Outrageous Fortune*, and Bluefield College's *Bluestone Review*. Her inspiration is West Virginia's Appalachian Mountains, where she writes in the majestic hills and works as a substitute teacher.

Laura Zucca-Scott is a college professor and writer. Her work has been published in English and Italian in many anthologies. She is interested in artistic expression and the transformative power of imagination.

www.ingramcontent.com/pod-product-compliance
Lightning Source LLC
Chambersburg PA
CBHW051718090426
42738CB00010B/1973